# ACTUAL SIZE

## by Steve Jenkins

pygmy shrew, 2 inches long

sandpiper

HOUGHTON MIFFLIN HARCOURT
BOSTON ★ NEW YORK

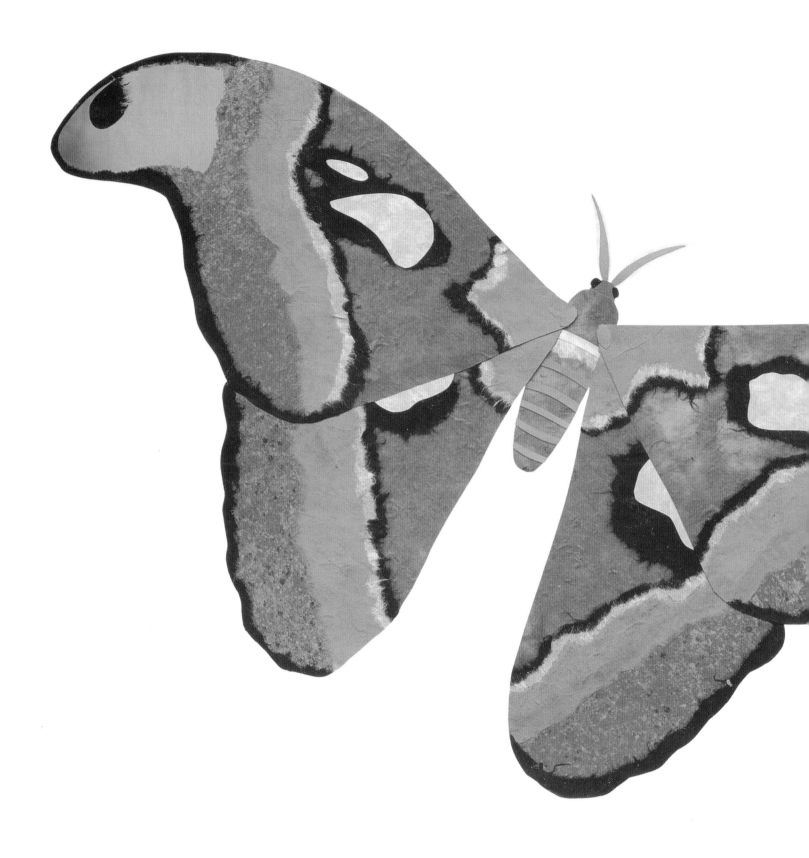

The **atlas moth** is so large that it is
often mistaken for a bird.

wingspan: 12 inches

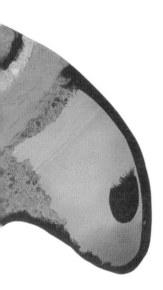

**D**id you ever look a giant squid in the eye? Have you shaken hands with a gorilla or been face to face with a tiger? All of the animals in this book are shown at actual size, so you can see how you measure up to creatures both large and small.

The **dwarf goby** is the smallest of all fish.

length: ⅓ inch

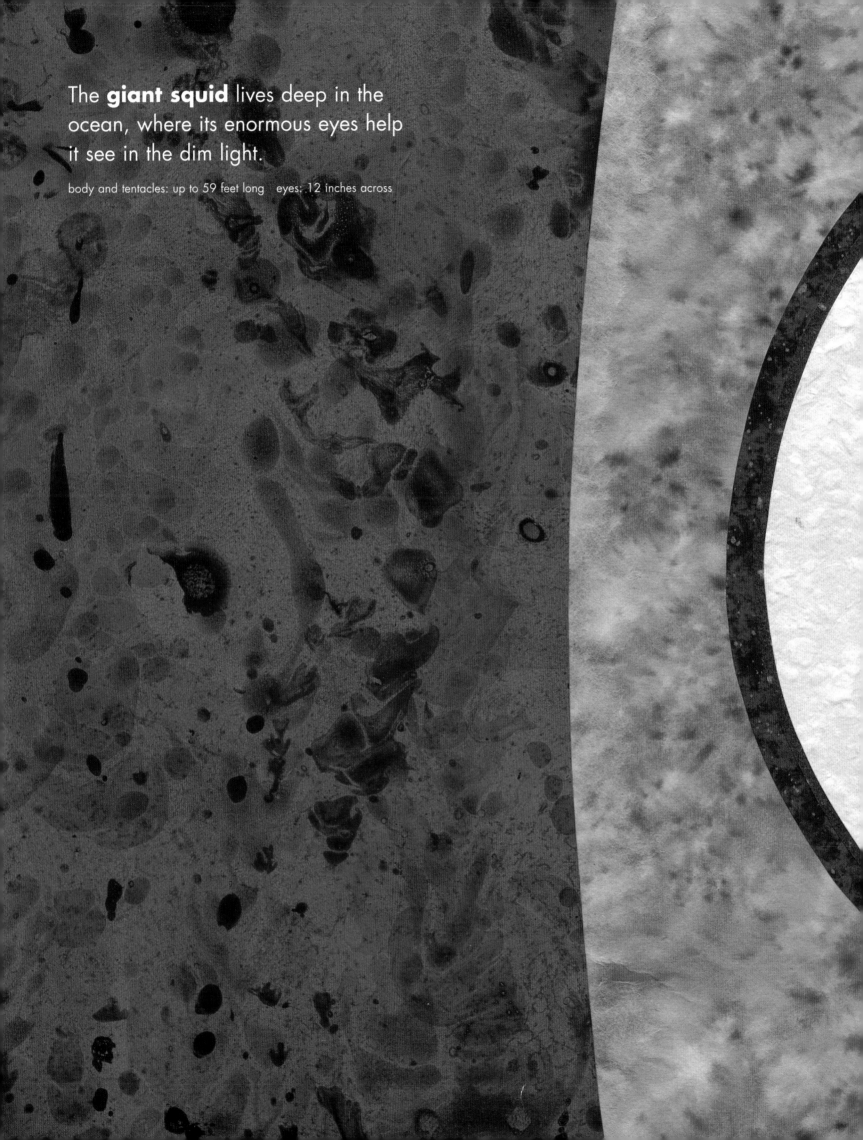

The **giant squid** lives deep in the ocean, where its enormous eyes help it see in the dim light.

body and tentacles: up to 59 feet long   eyes: 12 inches across

The **Alaskan brown bear** is the largest
meat-eating animal that lives on land.

height: 13 feet   weight: 1,700 pounds

Here's the largest bird—an **ostrich**—
with its egg.

height: up to 9 feet   weight: 340 pounds

A two-foot-long tongue! This must be a
**giant anteater** snacking on its favorite
food, termites.

body and tail: 7 feet long   weight: 85 pounds

The **Goliath birdeater tarantula** is big enough to catch and eat birds and small mammals.

legs: 12 inches across

The **saltwater crocodile**, the world's largest reptile, is a man-eater.

Length: 23 feet

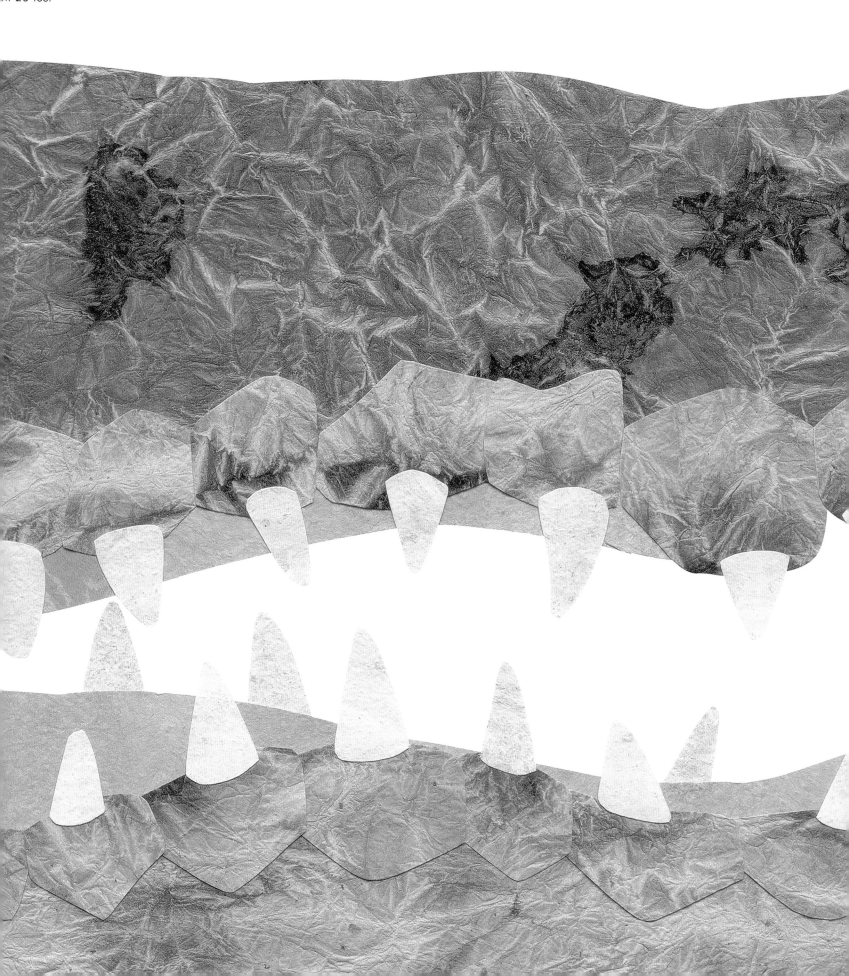

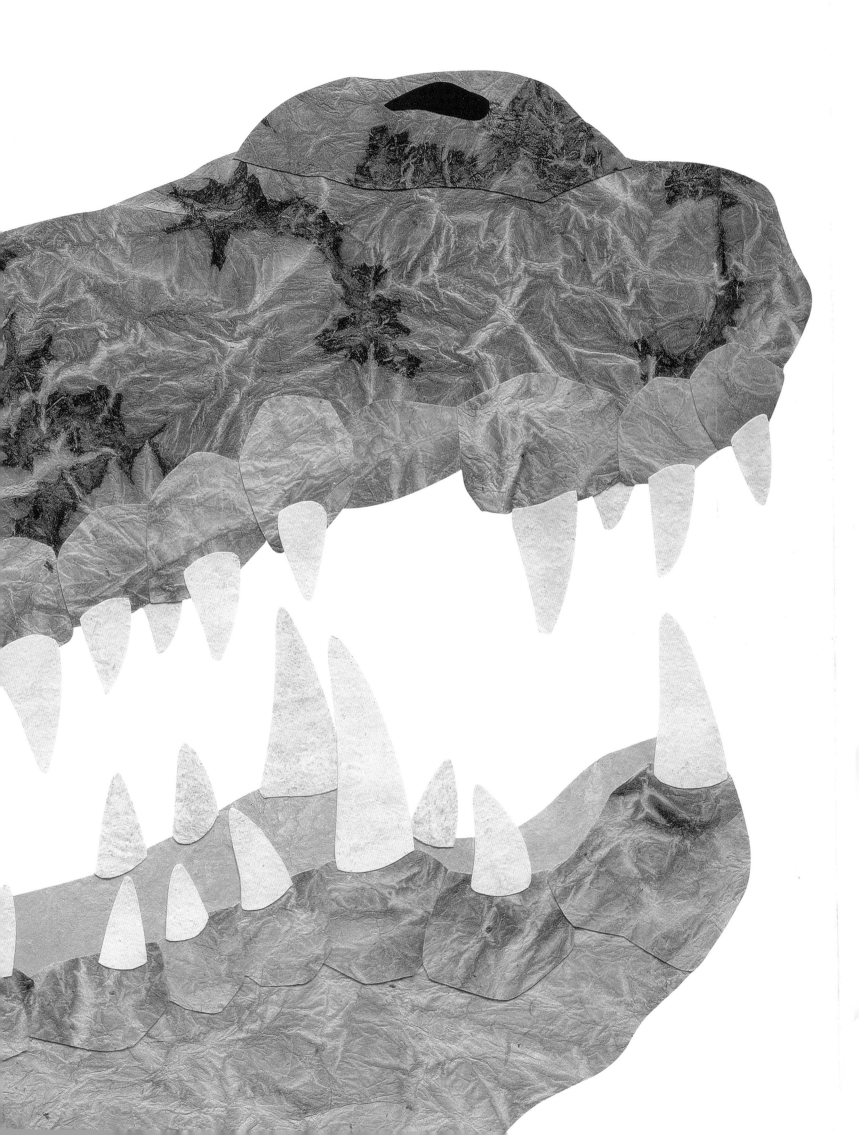

The **Goliath frog** lives in Africa. It's big
enough to catch and eat birds and rats.

length: 36 inches with legs extended   weight: 7 pounds

This is too close to a **great white shark!**

length: 21 feet   weight: 6,000 pounds   teeth: 4 inches long

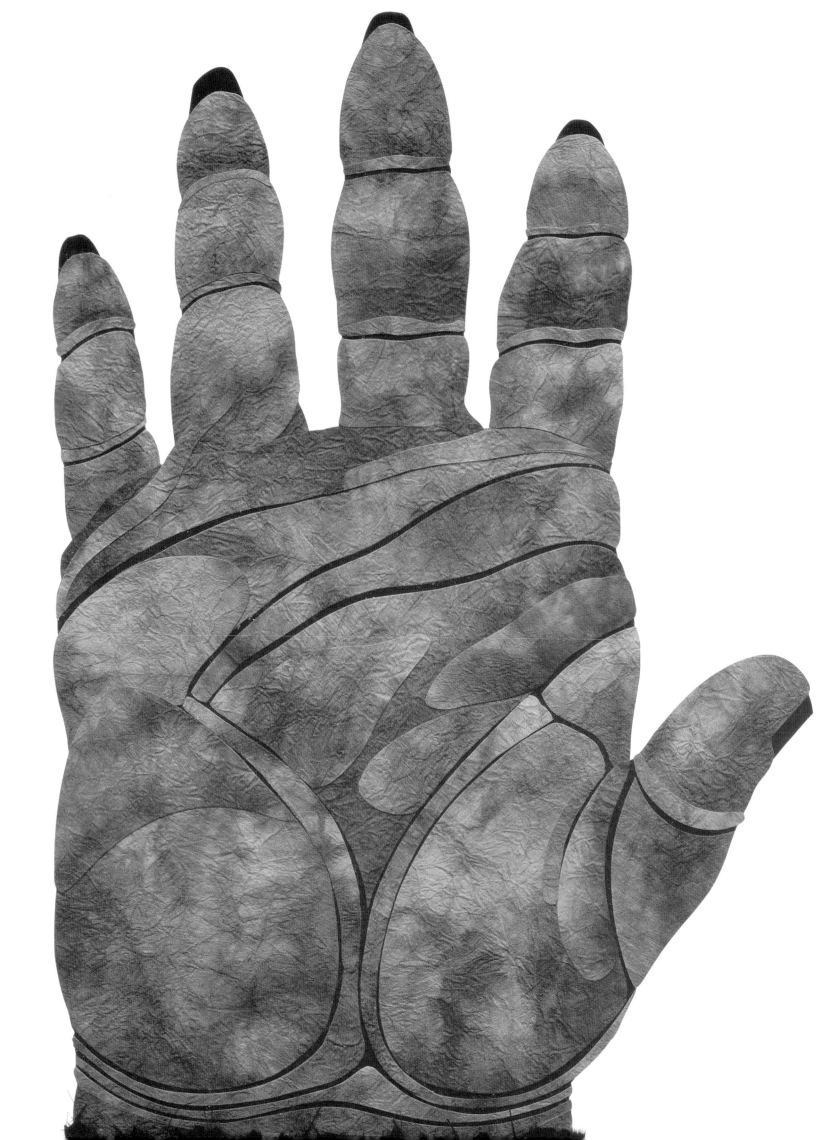

The huge **gorilla** and the **pygmy mouse lemur** both have hands a lot like ours.

gorilla: 5½ feet tall, 600 pounds    mouse lemur: 2½ inches tall, 1 ounce

The **Siberian tiger** is the biggest
of the big cats.

length: 14 feet, nose to tail   weight: 500 - 700 pounds

The **Goliath beetle** is the world's heaviest insect.

length: 6 inches   weight: 3½ ounces

The rare **giant walking stick** is the world's longest insect.

length: 22 inches

This foot belongs to the
largest land animal, the
**African elephant**.

height: up to 13 feet
weight: as much as 14,000 pounds

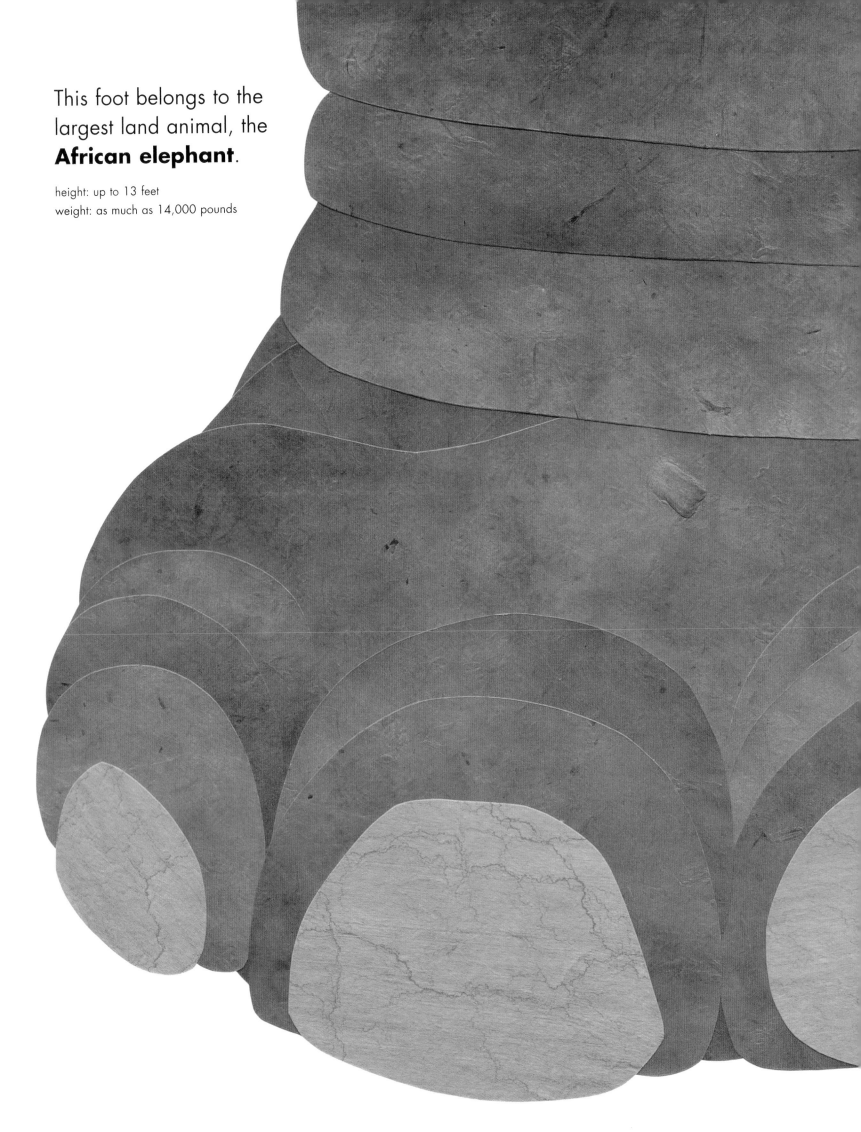

The **pygmy shrew** has a body just two inches long and weighs less than a dime. This tiny rodent lives in the mountains and forests of North America. The pygmy shrew consumes twice its own weight in food each day and is a fierce predator. It will eat almost anything it can catch and kill, including earthworms, insects, spiders, and small frogs.

The **giant squid** is a mysterious creature that has never been seen alive. The largest giant squid ever recorded was found dead in the waters off New Zealand. With its tentacles, it measured 59½ feet long and weighed more than one ton (2,000 pounds). These animals are relatives of the octopus and live in water 700 to 3,000 feet deep, where they probably eat fish, shrimp, and other squid that they capture with their two long feeder tentacles. They bite their prey into small pieces with a large, parrotlike beak. Giant squid have eyes the size of basketballs, the largest of any animal. Giant squid are a favorite food of sperm whales. The whales and squid must have terrific battles deep in the ocean—sperm whales are often found with huge round scars caused by the suckers on the squid's tentacles.

The **atlas moth** got its name because the patterns on its wings reminded people of maps. It is the largest moth, with wings up to 12 inches across. The atlas moth lives in Southeast Asia, where its large cocoons are sometimes made into pocket purses by the local people. The black spots on the tips of the atlas moth's wings are called eye spots. They make the wing tips look like snake heads, which may scare away predators. These moths do not feed. They have no mouth parts for eating, and they live only a few days.

Growing to about a third of an inch in length, the **dwarf goby**, the world's smallest fish, lives in the coral reefs of the western Pacific Ocean. It would take 7,000 dwarf gobies to weigh one ounce. Female gobies attach their eggs to coral or rocks, where the males guard them until they hatch.

The largest meat-eating animal that lives on land is the **Alaskan brown bear**. When it stands on its hind legs, it can be more than 13 feet tall, and it weighs as much as 1,700 pounds. Despite its size, this bear can run 35 miles per hour for short distances—faster than a horse. It makes its home in the arctic regions of the world and eats seeds, berries, insects, and small mammals. Sometimes brown bears eat larger animals, such as elk or moose. The Alaskan brown bear's favorite food is salmon, which it catches by standing in fast-moving rivers and grabbing the fish in its jaws or swatting them up onto the bank with its huge paws.

The **ostrich** can't fly, but it can run at speeds of over 40 miles per hour. Standing up to nine feet tall and weighing 340 pounds, it is the largest living bird. Ostriches live in groups, or flocks, which often mingle with herds of zebras and other grazing animals in Africa. The herds stir up the insects and small mammals that the ostriches eat, and the ostriches warn of approaching lions or hyenas. If necessary, the ostrich can defend itself against predators with powerful kicks of its legs. The ostrich egg, which weighs almost three and a half pounds, is the largest egg of any animal.

The **giant anteater** has no teeth in its long, narrow mouth. It uses its sticky two-foot-long tongue to eat up to 30,000 ants or termites a day, crushing them against the roof of its mouth. This anteater has long, curved claws on its front feet that it uses to tear open insect nests. It doesn't completely destroy the colonies of the insects it attacks, though, leaving enough ants or termites behind to rebuild their nests. Including its bushy tail, the giant anteater is six to eight feet in length and weighs up to 85 pounds. Giant anteaters make their home in the forests and grasslands of Central and South America. They are a favorite food of jaguars, but can defend themselves by standing up on their back legs and striking out with their claws. Anteaters have poor vision but a very good sense of smell.

The **Goliath birdeater tarantula**, with legs that can span 12 inches, is the largest spider in the world. It lives in burrows in the soft floor of South American forests, leaping out to grab insects, frogs, lizards, birds, and small mammals. Like most spiders, it kills or paralyzes its prey by injecting venom with its fangs. Birdeaters sometimes bite people, but luckily for us their bite isn't serious—it causes only mild pain, like a bee sting. Spiders don't have teeth to tear up their prey. Instead, they drool digestive juices onto their victims, then suck up their meal. Birdeaters also have the ability, unusual among spiders, to make sound. They create a soft hissing sound by rubbing the hairs on their legs together. They can also defend themselves by releasing hairs from their body. These tiny hairs are very irritating to the skin, eyes, and mouth of other animals.

The **saltwater crocodile** is the world's largest reptile. It grows up to 23 feet long and weighs as much as a ton. Saltwater crocodiles, which can live in both fresh and salt water, are found in the rivers and coastal areas of Australia and Southeast Asia, where they eat fish, birds, monkeys, buffalo, and livestock. This crocodile will float motionless for hours, waiting for an animal to come to the water's edge. It then slips under the water and quietly swims toward its intended victim. When it's close enough, strokes of its powerful tail launch it from the water. The crocodile grabs its prey in its two-foot-long jaws and drags it back into the water, where the animal is held under until it drowns. Saltwater crocodiles can stay under water for more than an hour and have been seen swimming in the ocean as far as 600 miles from land. Along with their relatives the alligators, crocodiles kill more people around the world than any other animal.

The world's largest frog is the **Goliath frog** of western Africa. From nose to toes, this frog is almost three feet long. It weighs as much as seven pounds, about the same as a housecat. Goliath frogs eat insects, other frogs and amphibians, and sometimes small mammals. Like all frogs, they don't drink water—they absorb it through their skin. These frogs are silent. They have no vocal sac, so they can't croak.

Many people think the **great white shark** is the scariest animal on earth. This fierce predator can be more than 20 feet long and weigh 6,000 pounds. Though it has been known to attack and kill humans, it prefers to eat seals, sea lions, and fish. In fact, great whites that attack people often spit them out after taking a bite. They have as many as 3,000 teeth, which are arranged in several rows. When a tooth breaks or falls out, one from the next row moves up to take its place. The shark is an ancient animal—it has looked much the same for more than 400 million years. These efficient hunters have a very good sense of smell and use special organs to detect the electrical fields of fish and other animals.

The smallest primate (and one of the smallest mammals) is the **pygmy mouse lemur**. This rare tree-dwelling creature has a body only about two and a half inches long and weighs less than an ounce. It lives in the forests of Madagascar, an island off the eastern coast of Africa. Lemurs eat fruit, flowers, and nectar. They sleep during the day and are active at night, using their large eyes to help them feed and move about.

The **gorilla**, found in the forests of central Africa, is an endangered animal. People have shot and captured so many gorillas that they are in danger of becoming extinct in the wild. These gentle but powerful animals are the largest primates, a group that includes the lemurs, monkeys, and great apes. The males stand five and a half to six feet tall and can weigh as much as 600 pounds. Gorillas are very intelligent animals that live in tight-knit social groups. They are attentive parents, playing with their babies and teaching them how to find food and get along with others in their group. Gorillas are vegetarians, eating leaves, fruit, nuts, and roots.

**Siberian tigers**, the largest of all cats, are found in the forests of one small part of Russia. These tigers are in great danger of becoming extinct—there are only a few hundred left in the wild. Siberian tigers can be up to 14 feet long (including their tail) and weigh as much as 700 pounds. They are stealthy and powerful predators, able to leap 30 feet in a single bound. These tigers hunt wild pigs, deer, and elk, though they will eat frogs, snakes, and small mammals—even porcupines—if larger prey can't be found.

The **Goliath beetle** is the world's heaviest insect. Found in the rain forests of central Africa, it is as long as six inches and can weigh nearly a quarter of a pound. This beetle is harmless to humans and is often kept as a pet in Japan and other countries. It feeds on dead plant material and dung.

The largest animal living on land is the **African elephant**. Elephants are endangered—they have long been hunted for their ivory tusks, and much of the African forest and grassland where they live has been turned into farmland. A male African elephant can stand 13 feet tall at the shoulder and weigh as much as 14,000 pounds. These sensitive and intelligent animals live in groups and feed on grass, shrubs, and trees. An elephant eats several hundred pounds of vegetation a day and feeds almost constantly when not sleeping. One of the elephant's most unusual features is its long, sensitive trunk, which it uses to eat, drink, defend itself, and care for its young. With its trunk, an elephant can tear down a tree or pick up an egg without breaking it.

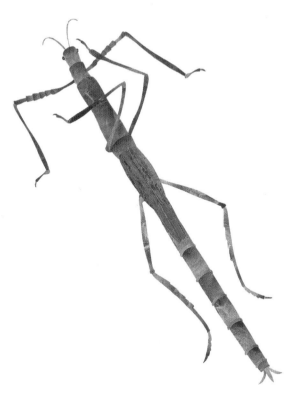

**Giant walking stick** insects are found in many parts of the world. The largest kind of giant walking stick is found in Indonesia, a group of islands in the western Pacific Ocean. One of these measured 22 inches long, easily making it the longest insect in the world. Walking sticks are gentle, slow-moving insects that feed on plants. When motionless, they look almost exactly like a twig or branch. This camouflage helps protect them from birds and other predators.

The world's largest earthworm can be found in one small part of Australia. The **giant Gippsland earthworm** grows to more than three feet in length and an inch in diameter. It lives in a complex system of burrows, where it eats roots and plant material in the soil. Earthworms move by stretching out the front of their body, then pulling up the back part. This motion creates a sucking noise that can be heard above the ground as the giant earthworm crawls through its underground tunnels.

*For Jamie*

All rights reserved. Published in the United States by Sandpiper, an imprint of Houghton Mifflin Harcourt Publishing Company. Originally published in hardcover in the United States by Houghton Mifflin Company, 2004.

SANDPIPER and the SANDPIPER logo are trademarks of Houghton Mifflin Harcourt Publishing Company.

For information about permission to reproduce selections from this book, write to trade.permissions@hmhco.com or to Permissions, Houghton Mifflin Harcourt Publishing Company, 3 Park Avenue, 19th Floor, New York, New York 10016.

www.hmhco.com

The text of this book is set in Futura.
The illustrations are collages of cut and torn paper.

The Library of Congress Cataloging-in-Publication Data is on file.

ISBN: 978-0-618-37594-3
ISBN: 978-0-547-51291-4 pa
Printed in China

SCP   20  19  18  17
4500738050

**The giant Gippsland earthworm** lives in Australia.

length: 36 inches